British Whales
Dolphins & Porpoises

British Whales

Dolphins & Porpoises

A guide

for the

identification and reporting

of

stranded Whales,

Dolphins and Porpoises

on the British coasts

BY

F. C. FRASER

BRITISH MUSEUM (NATURAL HISTORY)
LONDON: 1976

First Printed	.	.	.	.	1949
Second Edition	.	.	.	.	1953
Third Edition	.	.	.	.	1966
Fourth Edition	.	.	.	.	1969
Fifth Edition	.	.	.	.	1976

© British Museum (Natural History) 1976
Publication no. 549
ISBN 0 565 05549 6
BMNH/59.75/7.5m/3/76
Made in Great Britain by Burgess & Son (Abingdon) Ltd Abingdon Oxfordshire

PREFACE

The systematic reporting of stranded whales, dolphins and porpoises to the British Museum (Natural History) came into operation in 1913. The Keeper of Zoology at that time, Sir Sidney F. Harmer, K.B.E., F.R.S., was responsible for starting the scheme, and with the willing co-operation of the Board of Trade and other competent authorities a valuable supply of material and data has come to the Museum. By the end of 1974 a total of 1810 identifications of stranded cetaceans had been made. As might be expected many of the reports concerned commonly occurring species, but in addition it has become evident that certain other species thought to be rare are commoner than was previously believed and three species new to British waters have been recorded. The specimens sent to the Museum have been used to confirm identification; casts have been made from complete carcases for exhibition in the Whale Hall; anatomical dissections have been prepared from suitably fresh material; the national study collection has been greatly increased by the addition of many skulls and skeletons. The data about place, time and frequency of strandings are throwing light on aspects of the behaviour of cetaceans.

For the success of the arrangements acknowledgements are primarily due to the Department of Trade (and formerly the Board of Trade and Ministry of Transport). Receivers of Wreck and the Officers of the Coastguard Service have been mainly responsible for sending in reports and carcases or portions of carcases to the Museum. Generally the bulk and weight of whales and dolphins is considerable, decomposition after death is rapid, and not infrequently the place of stranding is almost inaccessible. Nevertheless the detailed reports (and when asked for, the specimens) received indicate the willing compliance of those on the coast involved. The Royal Scottish Museum, The Department of Lands and Fisheries and the National Museum of Ireland, Dublin, and many private individuals interested in marine mammals have also rendered valuable help.

This booklet has been produced primarily for the information of Receivers of Wreck and Officers of the Coastguard Services. However, its popularity with members of the public as a concise guide to the cetaceans occurring in British waters has made a reprint necessary and the opportunity has been taken of making use of a new set of illustrations prepared for the Museum by Elizabeth Sutton. The text remains as in the fourth edition.

J. G. SHEALS
Keeper of Zoology

February 1976

CONTENTS

INTRODUCTION

Cetaceans (the general name for whales, dolphins and porpoises), are mammals especially modified for the needs of an aquatic existence. With the change to a watery environment they have lost many of the characteristics of land mammals and have assumed, superficially at least, features which have led to their being confused with fishes.

Cetaceans are air-breathing, warm-blooded creatures; the developing young one is carried within the body of the mother for a period of months and when born is suckled for a further period until able to fend for itself. The cetacean's body has almost, but not entirely, lost the typical hairy covering of land mammals. In young animals especially a residue of hairs may still be found on the chin and snout. To maintain the body heat there is an insulating layer of fat, called *blubber*, immediately underneath the outer skin.

In accordance with their fish-like mode of life the body of whales and dolphins has become streamlined, all structures likely to impede the even flow of water over it have disappeared. In this process the hind limbs have been lost, although traces of their bony skeleton may still be found within the body. The head passes imperceptibly into the trunk without visible neck or shoulders. The nostrils, opening by a single or double *blowhole*, are situated on the top of the head and are generally remote from the muzzle. External ears are absent, but two small openings, one on each side of the head, lead into the organs of hearing. These minute apertures can generally be found by looking a little way above the middle point on the line from the eye to the insertion of the fore limb. The fore limbs, the *flippers*, have the same bony structure as that of any land mammal— upper arm, fore arm, wrist and finger bones—but they are modified into paddles and the fingers are enclosed within a common integument. Articulation at the wrist and elbow is not possible, the limb moves as a unit from the joint at the shoulder blade.

In most species there is a fin, the *back fin*, more or less triangular in shape and composed only of skin and fibrous tissue, situated at or behind the middle of the back. The body tapers towards the tail at the end of which it expands into a *horizontal* tail fin, the *flukes*. As in the dorsal fin the flukes are composed of skin and fibrous tissue without any supporting bony skeleton.

The male organ (penis) is often completely retracted, but the aperture of the cavity in which it lies is situated at a considerable

ix

distance from the vent, whereas the female reproductive opening is not far in front of the vent. The measurement of the distance between the two apertures gives thus an indication of the sex of the animal.

On each side of the reproductive opening in the female is a slit in the skin containing a teat, which may not be discovered unless it is looked for.

Note by Department of Trade

ROYAL FISH

England, Wales and Northern Ireland

Royal Fish, i.e. whales, porpoises, dolphins and sturgeons, whether dead or alive, belong to the Crown except where the carcase is washed ashore or stranded within the limits of a Manor in respect of which the title to Royal Fish has passed from the Crown to the Lord of the Manor. The liability for disposal or burial of carcases belonging to the Crown rests with the Department of Trade.

Scotland

In Scotland whales of the species known as "Bottle-nose" and "Caa'ing" and also whales of a length less than 25 feet from the snout or beak to the middle of the tail, belonging to any other species, including porpoises and dolphins, are not Royal Fish and should not be claimed on behalf of the Crown.

Receivers of Wreck and Officers of H.M. Coastguard should always endeavour so far as possible, to render assistance to the Museum Authorities in respect of all cetaceans, whether Royal Fish or not, by giving early information of strandings and any other services which it may be in their power to render to the Museum. No action should be taken, however, which would commit the Department of Trade to any liability in connection with the burial or disposal of carcases which are not Royal Fish, and specimens for transmission to the Museum should not be secured without the concurrence of the party responsible for burial (i.e. the persons claiming the carcase or the local Sanitary Authority).

THE REPORTING OF STRANDED WHALES DOLPHINS AND PORPOISES TO THE BRITISH MUSEUM (NATURAL HISTORY)

Receivers of Wreck and Officers of H.M. Coastguard are requested to give particular attention to the points indicated below, in reporting stranded Whales, Porpoises, etc., to the British Museum*

A *telegram* should be sent, making use of the registered address of the Museum (Nathismus Southkens London), and should, if possible, contain information with regard to the kind of Whale reported. The figures and descriptions on pages 10 to 34 may be used for finding this out.

The telegram should state where the animal was found (including the County, etc., if the place is a small one) and on what date, and it should give some of the characters which are most valuable in distinguishing one kind of Whale or Dolphin from another, particularly:

(*a*) Total length;

(*b*) Presence of whalebone *or* of teeth in the mouth;

(*c*) Colour of whalebone (if any);

(*d*) Number of teeth (if any), *of one side*, of upper and lower jaws, and their greatest diameter;

(*e*) Shape of beak or head, stating whether resembling one of Figs. 8 to 31;

(*f*) Colour of skin; if not all alike, with a note of the arrangement of dark and white parts on the body or head.

The following specimen telegrams will indicate the kind of information which is specially wanted:

[Telegram.] NATHISMUS SOUTHKENS LONDON.
"Whalebone whale thirty feet Pabbay Hebrides August 15 whalebone yellow white patch on flipper head Fig. 4."

[Telegram.] NATHISMUS SOUTHKENS LONDON.
"Toothed whale eighteen feet Penzance July 1 colour black teeth ten upper ten lower diameter three-eighths inch flippers four feet head Fig. 22."

If the kind of whale has been made out with the help of this pamphlet, its name should be indicated in the telegram thus:—
Lesser Rorqual instead of "Whalebone Whale", in the first telegram; or *Pilot Whale* instead of "Toothed Whale", in the second.

*It would be appreciated if members of the public would report strandings to the nearest Coastguard or Receiver of Wreck.

It is of great assistance to have a WRITTEN REPORT (on Form 136, supplied by the Museum) posted immediately after sending the telegram. This Report should contain answers to the following questions. If Form 136 is not available the questions may be referred to by their numbers only:

1. Is the tail horizontal, as in Figs. 2 and 3?

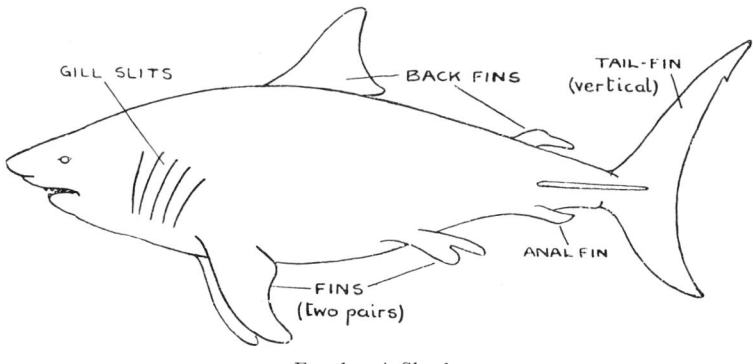

FIG. 1.—A Shark.

[If the tail is vertical, as in an ordinary fish, the specimen is probably a Shark, and *need not be reported.*

Some of the differences between a Shark and a Toothed Whale will be seen by comparing Fig. 1 with Fig. 2. A shark has 5-7 gill-slits, containing gills like those of an ordinary fish; a rough skin; two pairs of fins on the lower side; and several rows of teeth, one behind the other, in each jaw.

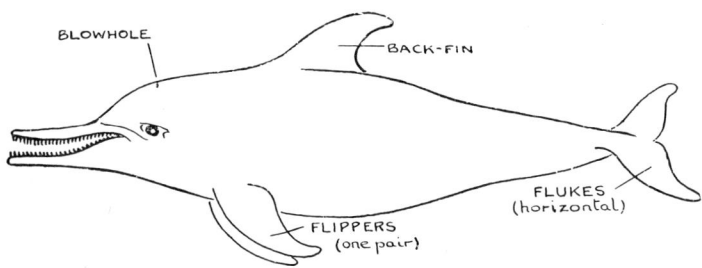

FIG. 2.—A small Toothed Whale or Dolphin.

In a Whale or Porpoise gill-slits are not present; the skin is smooth; there is only one pair of fins, flippers or paddles, on the sides of the body; and there is never more than one row of teeth on each side of each jaw, although teeth may be completely absent.]

2. Is there a hole ("blowhole") on the top of the head?

[All Whales and Porpoises have a hole, or two holes close together, for breathing air, in the middle line of the top of the head (Fig. 3), usually at some distance from the end of the snout.]

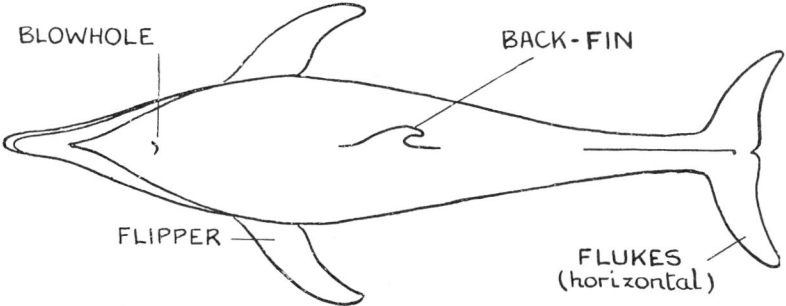

FIG. 3.—Back view of a Toothed Whale, showing the blowhole and the horizontal tail

3. Does the mouth contain whalebone?

4. If whalebone is present, state:

    (a) The colour of the whalebone-plates, and whether all of one colour;

    (b) The colour of its hairy fringes.

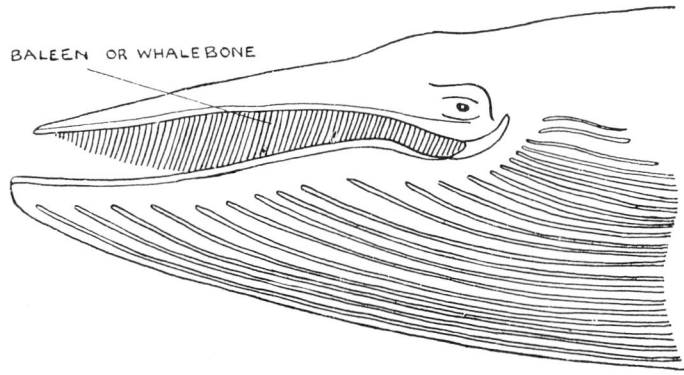

FIG. 4.—Head of Rorqual, a Whalebone Whale, showing the whalebone or baleen of one side in place and the grooves on the skin of the throat.

5. Is the skin of the throat marked by numerous deep grooves, as in Fig. 4?

    [Furrows of this kind are present in most Whalebone Whales, namely in the Humpback and in the Finners or Rorquals.]

3

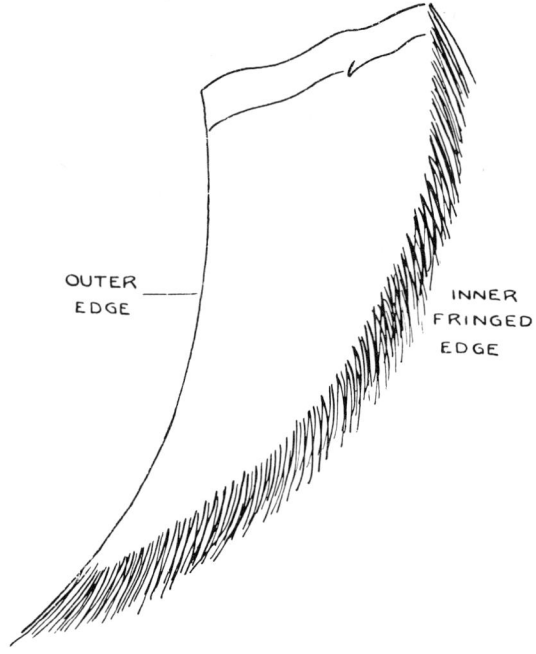

OUTER EDGE

INNER FRINGED EDGE

Fig. 5.—A single plate of whalebone or baleen, showing the hairy fringe.

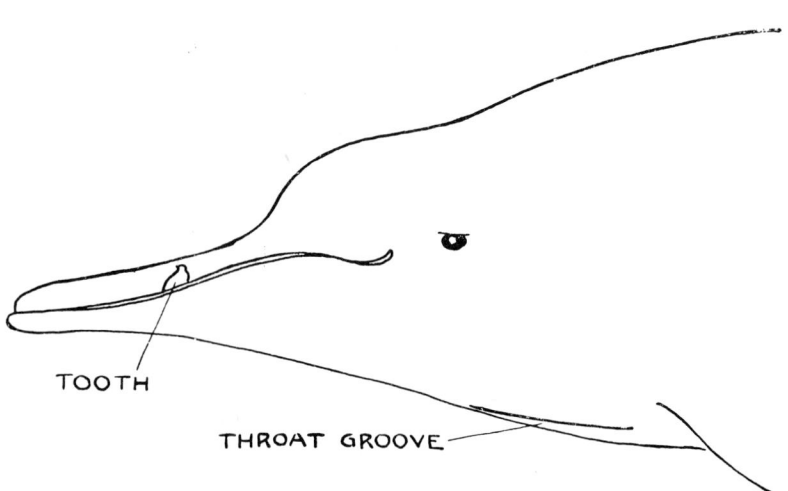

TOOTH

THROAT GROOVE

Fig. 6.—Head of a male Sowerby's Whale, in which only two teeth are present, one on each side of the lower jaw. In the females and young of this species the teeth are concealed beneath the gum, and none is visible.

4

6. Does the mouth contain teeth or do teeth seem to have been lost by decay?

7. If teeth are present, state:

(*a*) Whether they occur in both jaws or in the lower jaw only;
(*b*) The number of teeth, *of one side*, in the upper jaw;
(*c*) The number of teeth, *of one side*, in the lower jaw;
(*d*) If their number is very small, the position of the teeth in the jaw;
(*e*) The diameter of one of the largest teeth.
(*f*) Whether spade-shaped.

8. *If neither teeth nor whalebone can be found*, state whether the two halves of the lower jaw are:

(*a*) Arched outwards and widely separated half-way back in the jaw (in this case the specimen is a Whalebone Whale, and the whalebone has been washed out); *or*
(*b*) Close together at and near the front of the jaw, which is accordingly narrow (Toothed Whales in which the teeth are concealed beneath the gum).

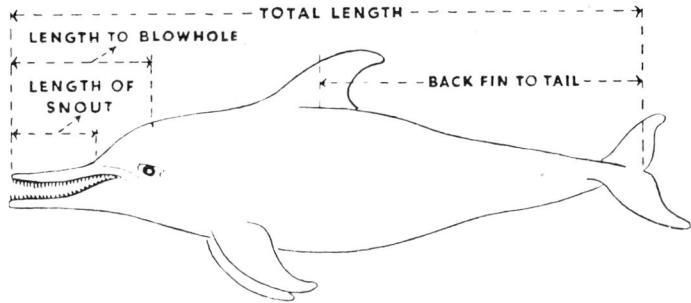

Fig. 7.—Side view of a Dolphin to show how the principal measurements should be taken.

9. Total length of the animal, measured in a straight line.

10. Length from the middle of the base of the back fin to the middle of the tail.

11. Length, *in the middle line*, of the snout or beak, if present.
   [The beak is a narrow portion of the front end of the upper jaw, usually separated by a line from the rest of the head, as in Figs. 3 and 7. In certain kinds, as in the common Porpoise, no beak can be distinguished.]

12. Length from the tip of the snout to the blowhole.

13. Length of one of the two flippers or paddles (see Fig. 2.)

14. Vertical height of the back fin, if present.

5

15. Shape of the head (for instance, "beak absent", or "beak six inches long, forehead much swollen"), referring to any figure in this leaflet which it seems to resemble.

16. Colour of the skin, calling attention to the position of any white parts observed.

17. Distance from the middle of the reproductive opening to the middle of the vent as an indication of the sex (see Introduction).

18. Is the specimen in good condition?
(If not, state the nature of the injuries.)

19. Is it lying in such a position that it could be secured for the Museum, if wanted, either entire, or its head, flippers, or complete skeleton?

A rough sketch of a side view of the animal is of great assistance in determining the kind of Whale which has been stranded.

Until a telegram has been received stating whether the specimen is required for the Museum, it is desirable to take steps to preserve it from mutilation or other injury.

The parts which are most likely to be required are the head and paddles. Even if the skin is damaged the bones may be in good enough condition to be worth securing.

The species of Whalebone Whales can be distinguished from one another by the characters of the whalebone or baleen. Receivers of Wreck and Coastguard Officers are accordingly requested to forward a single plate of baleen (see Fig. 5), from each such Whale found stranded. In most cases it would be advantageous to have this done as soon as possible after the discovery of the specimen.

Entire specimens, or certain parts, of the following kinds of Whales are specially likely to be required for the Museum: Sowerby's Whale, Cuvier's Whale, True's Beaked Whale, Narwhal, White Whale, False Killer, Risso's Dolphin, White-sided Dolphin, Euphrosyne Dolphin, Pigmy Sperm Whale.

In addressing specimens to the Museum use must not be made of the registered address (Nathismus Southkens London), which should be employed only for telegrams. Specimens sent either by post or by rail should be addressed:

THE KEEPER OF ZOOLOGY,
BRITISH MUSEUM (NATURAL HISTORY),
CROMWELL ROAD,
LONDON, S.W.7.

If any part of the flesh is sent it should be dispatched by the quickest route; and some disinfectant (formalin, salt, etc.), may with advantage be rubbed over the skin.

1 {
Whalebone present on palate. Teeth absent. Lower jaw very wide, its
halves arched outwards . . . **(Whalebone Whales)** 2
Whalebone absent. Teeth present, though sometimes concealed beneath
the gum. Lower jaw narrow, at least in front **(Toothed Whales)** 7

WHALEBONE WHALES

2 {
Lower surface of throat not grooved. No back fin. Mouth and upper
border of lower lip much arched. Whalebone blades long, up to
6–9 feet . . . . . . **Atlantic Right Whale**
Lower surface of throat with numerous parallel grooves . . . 3

3 {
Flippers extremely long, nearly one-third the length of the animal,
sometimes white externally, with a scalloped lower margin **Humpback**
Flippers much less than one-third the total length, not scalloped below
(Rorquals) 4

4 {
Whalebone, yellowish white or slate-coloured, or both . . . 5
Whalebone, black or nearly black 6

5 {
Size, up to 70 feet. Whalebone, yellow and slate-coloured, except at the
front of the right side, where it is white; its hairy fringes, white or
yellowish. Tail-flukes white below . . **Common Fin Whale**
Size, up to 30 feet. Whalebone and its hairy fringes, all white or yellowish.
A white region on outer side of flipper . . **Lesser Rorqual**

6 {
Size, up to 85 feet. Whalebone very black, with coarse black hairs
Blue Whale
Size, up to 50 feet. Whalebone mostly dark, with very fine, white,
curling, silky hairs, Tail-flukes not white below . . **Sei Whale**

TOOTHED WHALES

7 {
Tip of lower jaw well behind foremost limit of head 8
Tip of lower jaw at about same level as tip of snout 9

8 {
Size that of a large whale to about 60 feet . **Sperm Whale**
Size that of a dolphin to about 12 feet . **Pigmy Sperm Whale**

9 {
Back fin absent 10
Back fin present 11

10 {
Head short, with prominent "forehead". Colour greyish, with black
spots or mottlings. Either without visible teeth (females), or with a
tusk-lie tooth, several feet long, spirally twisted, projecting forwards
from the front of the upper jaw (males), exceptionally with two spiral
tusks . . . . **Narwhal**
Colour, white all over (greyish-brown in young individuals), 8–10 pairs
of teeth in each jaw . . . . . . **White Whale**

11 {
Teeth confined to the lower jaw, or apparently absent . . . 12
Teeth in both jaws 16

12 {
Back fin large, near middle of body. Teeth 2–7 pairs, at front end of
lower jaw . . . . **Risso's Dolphin**
Back fin considerably behind middle of body. Front end of jaws narrow.
Two grooves on throat . **(Whales of the "Bottle-nosed" type)** 13

*In using this key the enquirer should in all cases begin with the first bracket
(1), and should decide between the two alternatives there presented. He will
thus be referred either to bracket 2 or to bracket 7; and by continuing the process
of deciding between two alternatives he will sooner or later arrive at a definite
result. Suppose that a large whale with very strong teeth in its lower jaw, has
been found: of the two alternatives given in the first bracket, the second must be
chosen because teeth are present. The enquirer is thus referred to bracket 7, the
consideration of which shows at once that the specimen must be a Sperm Whale.

7

<table>
<tbody>
<tr><td rowspan="2">13</td><td>Size large, up to 25–30 feet. Distance from tip of snout to blowhole one-fifth to one-seventh the total length. "Forehead" very prominent. Teeth (one to two pairs) at tip of lower jaw, usually concealed
Bottle-nosed Whale</td><td></td></tr>
<tr><td>Distance from tip of snout to blowhole less than one-seventh the total length . . . .</td><td>14</td></tr>
</tbody>
</table>

13 { Size large, up to 25–30 feet. Distance from tip of snout to blowhole one-fifth to one-seventh the total length. "Forehead" very prominent. Teeth (one to two pairs) at tip of lower jaw, usually concealed
Bottle-nosed Whale
Distance from tip of snout to blowhole less than one-seventh the total length 14

14 { Size, large, up to 26 feet. Distance from tip of snout to blowhole one-tenth to one-eighth the total length. "Forehead" not specially prominent. Teeth one pair at tip of lower jaw, massive in males (diameter 1 inch), concealed in females . . . . . **Cuvier's Whale**
Size smaller, not exceeding 20 feet. Beak long 15

15 { Length about 15 feet. Colour mostly black, usually with white marks. One pair of teeth at middle of length of lower jaw, conspicuous and triangular in males, concealed in females . **Sowerby's Whale**
Size rather larger. Colour not satisfactorily known. One pair of teeth at tip of lower jaw, conspicuous and flattened sideways in males, concealed in females . . . . **True's Beaked Whale***

16 { Size large, 15–30 feet in adults. Teeth 8–13 in each jaw . . . 17
Seldom exceeding 12 feet, usually less than 9 feet. Teeth not more than ½ inch in diameter, more than 15 pairs 19

17 { "Forehead" greatly swollen, overhanging the tip of the very short beak. Flippers narrow, about one-fifth of the total length. Colour black, with only a small amount of white on lower surface. Teeth 8–12 pairs in each jaw, less than ½ inch in diameter . . **Pilot Whale**
"Forehead" not prominent. Teeth, 10–13 pairs in each jaw, at least ¾ inch in diameter 18

18 { Colour conspicuously black and white (or yellow). Flippers broad, not pointed. Teeth about 1 inch in diameter . . . **Killer**
Colour black all over. Flippers narrow and pointed. Teeth as in the Killer . . . . **False Killer**

19 { Size up to 5½ feet. Teeth about 21–24 pairs in each jaw, flattened sideways, with spade-shaped crowns. Beak not distinguishable . .
Common Porpoise
Size larger, teeth conical, the crowns not flattened sideways. Beak distinct 20

20 { Length up to 12 feet. Beak about 3 inches long in middle line. Teeth large, 20–25 pairs in each jaw; diameter, ⅜–½ inch . . . .
Bottle-nosed Dolphin
Teeth not exceeding ¼ inch in diameter 21

21 { Beak about 2 inches long in middle line. Length, 9–10 feet . . 22
Beak up to 6 inches in middle line. Teeth, 40–50 pairs in each jaw, about 1/10 inch in diameter. Length up to 7 feet 23

22 { Upper lip white. Dark colour of flippers continuous with that of body, their lower margin not much curved. Teeth, about 25 pairs in each jaw; diameter, ¼ inch . . . **White-beaked Dolphin**
Upper lip black. Flippers, with strongly curved lower margin, arising from white part of body, usually connected with dark part by a narrow dark streak. A conspicuous white region on each side, behind the back fin. Teeth, 30–40 pairs in each jaw; diameter, 3/16 inch . . .
White-sided Dolphin

23 { A well-marked, narrow dark band of pigment extending from the eye along the flank and curving down to the vent, with a subsidiary branch in the region of the flipper insertion . . **Euphrosyne Dolphin**
This band wanting, but an arrangement of yellowish, white and dark bands on the sides of the body . . . **Common Dolphin**

---

*In addition to Sowerby's Whale and True's Beaked Whale, the two species of *Mesoplodon* mentioned in bracket 14, it is probable that a third species (*M. europaeus*), perhaps reaching 20 feet in length, will be recorded as British. Its external appearance is not well known.

BRITISH WHALES, DOLPHINS AND PORPOISES

Cetaceans are divided into two groups, in one of which the mouth contains WHALEBONE or BALEEN; while in the other TEETH are present although sometimes concealed below the gum.

I. WHALEBONE WHALES

Each side of the palate carries a row of triangular, hairy plates, the baleen or whalebone blades. These are arranged transversely to the length of the palate and their free ends hang down into the cavity of the mouth. The inner edge of each is frayed out into a hair-like fringe, and all the fringes together form two sieve-like surfaces used to collect the small organisms which form the food of whalebone whales. The kind of whale can be determined by the colour of the blades and of their hairy fringes.

In all the Whalebone Whales the blowhole is paired, it is in the form of two longitudinal slits on the top of the head.

NORTH-ATLANTIC OR BISCAYAN
RIGHT WHALE
Balaena glacialis Bonnaterre

Length.—Up to 60 feet.

Colour.—General colour completely black all over but occasionally irregular white patch on belly.

Form.—Head about a quarter of total length. Upper jaw arched and narrow. Lower jaws forming scoop-shaped structure, the upper margin of the lip at side of jaw strongly curved upwards. Top of head, commonly with rough horny projection—the "Bonnet"; mouth region, barnacle-infested. Back fin entirely wanting. Tail flukes with notch in the middle of the hinder margin. Grooving on throat absent. Flippers large, rounded, much broader than in rorquals.

Baleen or *Whalebone.*—Largest blades may be 6 to 9 feet long. Much longer and narrower than in any other British whalebone whale. Colour black, with fringes of same colour.

General Remarks.—No Right Whales have stranded on the British coast since the reporting of stranded whales was instituted in 1913, but there are earlier records which undoubtedly involve this species. When whaling companies operated in the Hebrides the Biscayan Right Whale was not infrequently included in the catch. The majority were caught in June, and of sixty-seven recorded the largest measured 59 feet.

HUMPBACK WHALE
Megaptera novaeangliae (Borowski)

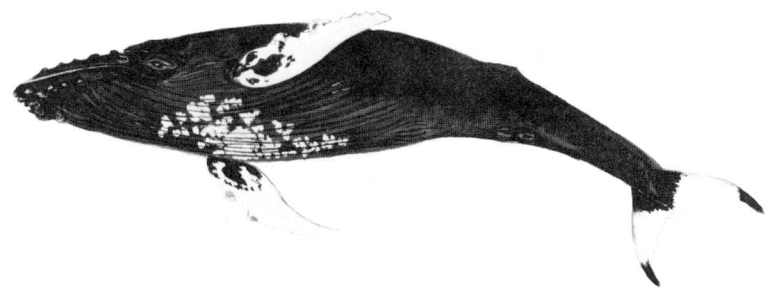

Length.—Up to about 50 feet.

Colour.—Black above, white below, but great individual variation in relative amounts of black and white present. Flippers white underneath, absence of pigment sometimes extending round forward edge onto upper surface. Flukes usually white underneath.

Form.—General form robust. Snout short, broad, with many tubercles on surface. Similar tubercles on chin and on sides of lower jaws. Back fin in hinder third of body, rather small, posterior border only shallowly concave, general shape rather variable. Flukes with hinder edge irregular and notch in middle. Flippers conspicuously long and narrow, front edge with numerous irregular knobs, quarter to one-third body length. Head, flippers and other parts usually infested with barnacles. Throat grooves much fewer and more widely spaced apart than in Blue and Fin Whales, extending to navel.

Baleen or *Whalebone.*—Largest blade about 3 feet long. Colour nearly black with fringes of same colour.

General Remarks.—This species has not been reported as stranding on the British coast since the records of stranded cetaceans were commenced in 1913. Nevertheless it was taken in British waters during the time that commercial whaling companies operated. An earlier record is from the Firth of Tay where a Humpback was observed for five or six weeks in 1883 before being harpooned and finally killed, its carcase being found floating off the coast of Kincardinshire.

11

COMMON RORQUAL OR FIN WHALE

Balaenoptera physalus (Linnæus)

Length.—Up to 80 feet, usually about 70 feet.

Colour.—Grey above white below. Head asymmetrically pigmented. Right lower jaw white, left pigmented on outside. Inner sides of flippers and under surface of flukes white.

Form.—General form long slender. Snout broad and low but outer margins forming an acute angle, not nearly parallel for most of their length as in Blue Whale. Back fin in hinder third of body, rather high, triangular with concave hinder edge. Tail flukes with notch in middle of hinder edge. Numerous parallel grooves on throat and chest ending very near umbilicus (navel).

Baleen or *Whalebone.*—Longest blade less than 3 feet long. Plates of *right* side usually white for two or three feet from front end. Remainder on right side and all left striped with alternating bands of yellow and slate-colour or bluish grey. Fringes of plates yellowish white.

General Remarks.—This species like the Blue Whale has a world-wide distribution, and also like the latter it undertakes extensive migrations between high and low latitudes. On the British coast strandings have been moderately frequent since records were commenced in 1913, although they have been much less often reported in the latter half of the period covered. The monthly figures are consistent with the view that the majority have been stranded either on their northward migration in the late winter and spring or on their southward migration in the autumn.

LESSER RORQUAL OR PIKE WHALE
Balaenoptera acutorostrata Lacépède

Length.—Up to 30 feet.

Colour.—General colour black above, pure white below from chin to tail flukes. Tail flukes white below. Flipper with conspicuous white patch on outer surface.

Form.—General form resembling the Fin Whale but rather stouter. Snout outline viewed from above distinctly triangular. Back fin, in hinder third of body, prominent, with backward projecting apex and concave posterior border. Flippers one-eighth body length, narrow, tapering to a rounded tip. Throat grooves numerous, ending posteriorly in front of the navel. Flukes with notch in middle of hinder edge.

Baleen or *Whalebone.*—Longest blade about one foot. All blades white or yellowish, with fringes of the same colour.

General Remarks.—This is a relatively common species on the British coasts, 106 strandings having been reported since 1913. These have occurred on all parts of the coast with the exception of the southern part of the North Sea and the English Channel from the Straits of Dover to Devonshire. The distribution of strandings suggest that this rorqual enters the North Sea round the north end of Scotland rather than by way of the Straits of Dover.

BLUE WHALE OR SIBBALD'S RORQUAL
Balaenoptera musculus (Linnæus)

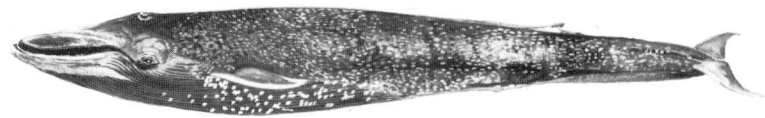

Length.—Up to 100 feet, usually about 85 feet.

Colour.—Dark bluish grey, the lower surface resembling the back in tint; speckled with white spots and pale mottling. Outer tip and under surface of flipper white.

Form.—Snout broad and low, flattened, not arched, edges of snout almost parallel to within a short distance of tip, where they curve round to meet. Flippers long and tapering with lower edges curved, about one-seventh body length. Back fin small, triangular, situated in hinder third of body length. Tail flukes with notch in middle of hinder edge. Under surface of throat scored longitudinally by numerous deep parallel grooves extending more than half-way towards the tail.

Baleen or *Whalebone.*—Longest blade not more than 3 feet long. Attached edge broad in proportion to length. Colour jet-black with hairy fringes of the same colour.

General Remarks.—Distribution is world-wide and extensive migrations between high and low latitudes, correlated with feeding and breeding are undertaken. Considerable numbers of Blue Whales were killed by the whaling companies which used to operate on the British coasts, but stranded specimens are very rare. Only four have been recorded since 1913, all of these prior to 1923.

SEI WHALE OR RUDOLPHI'S RORQUAL
Balaenoptera borealis Lesson

Length.—Up to 60 feet, usually about 50 feet.

Colour.—In general pigment symmetrical on either side of body. On the back bluish grey, somewhat lighter on undersurface. A white area confined to grooving on throat and chest but not extending on to chin, rather variable in size but never extending beyond the hinder end of the grooving. Tailwards of the grooving light grey. Under surfaces of flukes never white and under surface of flippers usually also pigmented.

Form.—Less slender than Fin Whale but still having graceful general proportions. Snout low and acutely pointed as in Fin Whale. Edge of snout viewed from side slightly arched. Back fin in hinder third of body, relatively larger than that of Blue or Fin Whales, apex projecting backward, pronounced concave hinder edge. Flippers small, about one-eleventh body length. Flukes with notch in middle of hinder edge. Throat grooves numerous, ending some distance in front of umbilicus.

Baleen or *Whalebone.*—Colour mostly black with fringes greyish white and very fine in texture. Frequently a few white blades at front end of series.

General Remarks.—The Sei Whale has only been recorded seven times since the reporting of stranded cetacea was started in 1913, the last occasion being in 1965. Like the Blue and Fin Whales it was an important constituent of the catch of the whaling companies which used to operate on the western seaboard of the British Isles. The whaling statistics indicate that the species is commoner than the number of stranded specimens would suggest. It is world-wide in distribution.

15

II.—TOOTHED WHALES

Whalebone is absent. Teeth are present in larger or smaller numbers, but if they are reduced to a single pair they are usually concealed beneath the gum in the females, or young of either sex, of the species concerned. Such specimens may be recognised as Toothed Whales by the shape of the lower jaw, which is narrow in front instead of being widely arched outwards as in Whalebone Whales. In recently born individuals of all kinds the teeth are uncut, while in old specimens they are commonly much worn down, and some may be missing. The number of missing teeth can often be estimated by careful examination.

In Toothed Whales the nostrils open by a single blowhole, crescentic in shape and placed high on the top of the head in all species except the Sperm Whales, in which it is situated on the side at the front of the head.

SPERM WHALE OR CACHALOT
Physeter catodon Linnæus

Length.—Males up to 60 feet, females about 30 feet.

Colour.—General colour very dark bluish grey, often gradually lightening on sides to restricted very light grey or white area on belly. Sometimes considerably lighter on under surface of head and lower jaw which latter may be white. "Forehead" with whorl of lighter and darker pigment flecks. White scars and circles on head of older animals.

Form.—Head enormous. Square in front and bearing a single blowhole on left side at front and top of head. Lower jaws shorter than rest of head, narrow and provided with numerous teeth, the exposed portions fitting into sockets in upper jaw when mouth closed. Back fin small, hump-like; between it and tail a succession of lesser humps. Rather larger hump behind vent. Body generally not smooth but irregularly corrugated. Short ill-defined furrows in throat region. Hinder margin of tail with notch in middle.

Teeth.—Twenty to thirty on each side of lower jaw. Number on each side not necessarily equal. Size of teeth as much as 8 in. long and $3\frac{1}{2}$ in. in transverse diameter. No functional teeth in upper jaw but small vestigial teeth not infrequent; usually placed internally to the sockets into which tips of lower teeth fit.

General Remarks.—The Sperm Whale, the largest of the toothed whales, is only rarely stranded on the British coasts. Since 1913 twelve reports have been received, for the most part they concerned old male animals. The Sperm Whale is a frequenter of warm equatorial waters, and it is almost exclusively the old males which extend their range into higher latitudes.

PIGMY SPERM WHALE OR LESSER CACHALOT
Kogia breviceps (Blainville)

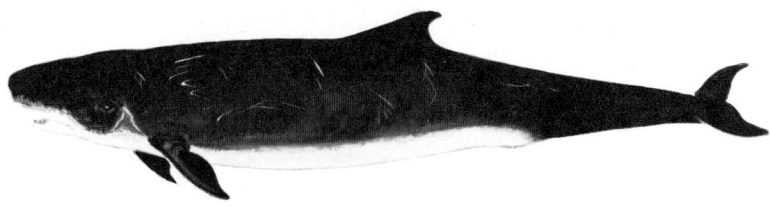

Length.—9 to 13 feet.

Colour.—Dark on back, white on under surface from area round mouth to tail. Both surfaces of flukes darkly pigmented. Flippers darkly pigmented but originating within white ventral area.

Form.— General form dolphin-like, rather robust. Head conical with mouth terminating four to six inches behind snout tip, giving animal some resemblance to a shark. Back fin situated just behind middle of body length, well defined, pointed, with shallowly concave hinder margin. Blowhole single, on left of middle line, crescentic, curving obliquely from mid line outward and backward with concavity turned forward and to left. Flippers broad but tapering to the tip. Flukes with notch in middle of hinder margin.

Teeth.—Normally confined to lower jaw, nine to fourteen on each side; very rarely a pair of upper jaw teeth. Teeth long, slender, curved; diameter about $\frac{1}{10}$ in.

General Remarks.—It was predicted that, sooner or later, the Pigmy Sperm Whale would be included in the list of stranded cetaceans as it had been recorded from Britanny and Holland since the beginning of the century. A specimen 8 ft $1\frac{1}{2}$ in. long was reported by the National Museum of Ireland in 1966. It was stranded near Lahinch, Co. Clare.

BOTTLE-NOSED WHALE*
Hyperoodon ampullatus (Forster)

Length.—Old males up to 30 feet, females 24 feet.

Colour.—Dark grey to black above, some grey or white on under surface. Flippers and flukes dark on both surfaces. Old animals may be white or yellow on front of head.

Form.—Prominently bulging "forehead" above well-defined beak measuring six to seven inches long in middle line. Distance from tip of snout to blowhole one-fifth to one-seventh body length. Back fin situated behind middle of body, rather small, with backwardly projecting apex and concave posterior margin. Tail flukes *without* notch in middle of hinder margin. Flippers small, narrow, tapering to a point. Two throat grooves approximating to each other and nearly meeting at front ends.

Teeth.—A single pair (occasionally two pairs) at tip of lower jaw. These concealed below gum in female so that mouth appears to be entirely toothless. Teeth oval in cross-section, in male at widest part about $\frac{3}{4}$ in. $\times$ $\frac{1}{2}$ in., in female somewhat less.

General Remarks.—The Bottle-nosed Whale is a fairly common species on the British coasts. Sixty-six records of stranding have been obtained since 1913. Strandings evenly distributed round the coast have been commonest in late autumn and winter, and their incidence is believed to be correlated with a migration southwards from the far north where they have spent the summer. The greater length of the snout tip to blowhole in this species is a convenient way of distinguishing it from allied species with which it is likely to be confused.

*This whale is not a "Royal Fish" *in Scotland*, and any carcase washed ashore *on that part of the British Islands* should not be buried at the expense of the Department of Trade.

CUVIER'S WHALE
Ziphius cavirostris (Cuvier)

Length.—Up to 26 feet.

Colour.—Inadequately known, further information required. Specimen stranded on Irish coast described thus: "The whole of the head, including the lower jaw, and part of the body were cream white, separated from the dark skin of the rest of the animal by an oblique line passing from the anterior end of the dorsal fin in front of the flipper to the posterior end of the lower jaw. Much of the skin was covered by long linear streaks . . .", but specimens dark above and light below have also been described.

Form.—General form rather stout. Profile of head passing gradually into that of beak, "forehead" less prominent than in Bottle-nosed Whale. Distance of snout from blowhole less than one-seventh total length. Back fin behind middle of body, forward edge slightly convex, hinder concave. No notch in middle of hinder edge of tail flukes. Flippers small. Two throat grooves as in *Hyperoodon*.

Teeth.—A single pair at the tip of lower jaw. In male visible above gum, diameter up to about 1¾ in. In female embedded in gum, not visible, more slender and tapering than in male.

General Remarks.—Until the systematic recording of stranded cetaceans was started, Cuvier's Whale was believed to be a rare species. Since 1913 the thirty-one reports of this animal indicate that it is not uncommon in British waters. All the strandings have been on the Irish coast or on the west coast of England and Scotland.

SOWERBY'S WHALE
Mesoplodon bidens (Sowerby)

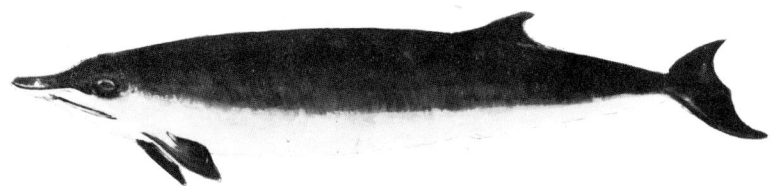

Length.—Up to 15 feet.

Colour.—Mostly black, often with irregular white blotches or streaks, sometimes white on belly. Scratches and marks on skin.

Form.—More slender than Cuvier's Whale. Beak slender passing gradually into receding "forehead". Distance from tip of snout to blowhole less than one-seventh total length of body. Back fin behind middle of body length, with slightly convex forward edge, concave hinder edge. No notch in middle of hinder margin of tail flukes. Flippers short, narrow, tapering to a bluntly rounded tip. Two throat grooves as in *Hyperoodon*.

Teeth.—Large, flattened, triangular tooth on each side of lower jaw near middle of its length, exposed in males, concealed in females.

General Remarks.—This is one of the rarer beaked whales in British waters, only twenty-one having so far been recorded since 1913. It is a North Atlantic species originally described from a specimen stranded in the Moray Firth in 1800. Its smaller size, slender snout and the position of the teeth help to distinguish it from Cuvier's Whale and the Bottle-nosed Whale.

TRUE'S BEAKED WHALE
Mesoplodon mirus True

Length.—About 17 feet.

Colour.—From the original description: "Back, slate black; lower sides, yellow purple, flecked with black; median line of belly somewhat darker; a greyish area in front of vent; fins the colour of black," but Irish specimen said to be black along the whole dorsal surface, the lower surface a very light colour approaching white, without any other markings.

Form.—Slender, body compressed on sides especially the tail stock. "Forehead" low. Back fin situated behind middle of body. Flippers small, inserted low down on the sides, tapering to a rounded tip. Two throat grooves approximating at front end, wide apart at hinder end. Blowhole single, crescentic. Tail flukes without notch in middle of hinder margin.

Teeth.—Two teeth at extreme front end of lower jaw. In males at least teeth more compressed or flattened than those of Cuvier's Whale. Teeth exposed in male, concealed below gum in female.

General Remarks.—This species, one of the rarest beaked whales, has been recorded only three times in British waters. Its external appearance is inadequately known and more information is required. The two species with which it might be confused because of the situation of the teeth at the tip of the lower jaw are the Bottle-nosed Whale and Cuvier's Whale. From the former True's Whale can be distinguished by the shape of the head—the "forehead" high and bulging in the Bottle-nosed Whale, the beak merging into a very receding "forehead" in True's Whale.

True's Whale differs from Cuvier's Whale in its smaller size and more slender body. The body colour may also give an indication of the species involved. If the animal being examined is a male the shape of the teeth will be a useful guide. In Cuvier's Whale the cross-section is circular; in True's, which has teeth flattened on the sides, the cross-section is an oblong with rounded ends.

NARWHAL
Monoceros monoceros Linnæus

Length.—Up to 16 feet.

Colour.—Greyish with numerous black spots or mottling, rather lighter on the sides and belly. Young animal bluish grey, darker than adult and without the mottling of the latter.

Form.—Head short, with conspicuous "forehead", not prolonged into a snout. No well-defined dorsal fin, in its place a ridge an inch or two in height extending along the middle of the back. Flippers small, broad, bluntly rounded. Flukes with notch in middle of hinder edge.

Teeth.—Two teeth in *upper* jaw. Completely concealed in females so that they appear toothless. In males the right tooth concealed, but the left, marked with anti-clockwise spiral, growing out at the front of the head as a conspicuous tusk several feet long. Very rarely both teeth thus developed.

General Remarks.—The Narwhal is confined in its distribution almost exclusively to Arctic Seas, but it has been recorded five times on the British coast, in the Firth of Forth, 1648; at Boston, Lincolnshire, 1800; at the Shetland Islands, 1808; and more recently, in 1949, two females, the one at Rainham, Essex, and the other in the Medway.

A tuskless Narwhal might be mistaken for a young White Whale (which however, has teeth in both jaws), but no other difficulty ought to be experienced, as in contrast to ordinary dolphins, these two species have no dorsal fin.

WHITE WHALE OR BELUGA
Delphinapterus leucas (Pallas)

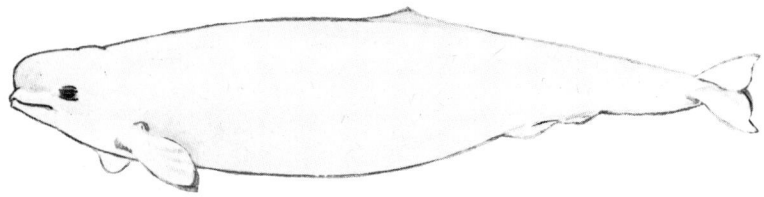

Length.—Up to 18 feet, generally 12 to 14 feet.

Colour.—Adult white or cream coloured-all over. Young animals greyish-brown becoming white when four or five years old.

Form.—Head without beak. No back fin. General shape as in Narwhal. Flippers of moderate size, broad, with a rounded edge. Flukes with notch in middle of hinder edge.

Teeth.—Eight to ten on each side of upper and lower jaws. Diameter in adult about $\frac{1}{2}$ in.; some of the teeth of young animals bear small lobular processes which become lost by wear.

General Remarks.—Like the Narwhal, the White Whale is a true Arctic species circumpolar in its distribution, and visits British waters only at infrequent intervals. Prior to 1913, when systematic recording of stranded cetaceans commenced, only nine instances of British strandings were known from the end of the eighteenth century. A young one was taken in the River Forth about twenty-five miles west of the Forth Bridge in 1932. The report concerning it stated that the teeth had not cut the gums but their tips could be felt through the skin. Such an indication would at once distinguish a young White Whale from a Narwhal with which it might otherwise be confused.

PILOT WHALE, BLACKFISH OR CAA'ING WHALE*

Globicephala melaena (Traill)

Length.—Up to 28 feet, generally about 20 feet.

Colour.—Black over most of the body. White area just behind chin well defined from surrounding black anteriorly but hinder margin less distinct and may extend as a white streak for some distance along belly.

Form.—General form long and slender. Bulging "forehead" above very short beak. Long, low back fin with tip backwardly projecting, situated about middle of the body length. Flippers very long and narrow, about one-fifth of the body length. Flukes with notch in middle of hinder edge.

Teeth.—Eight to ten on each side of upper and lower jaws. Diameter at gum nearly $\frac{1}{2}$ in.

General Remarks.—The general distribution of the Pilot Whale is to the north of the British Isles. It is common in the vicinity of the Faroe, Orkney and Shetland Islands, but is not infrequent farther south. The seventy-four recorded strandings involved numbers of animals ranging from single specimens to a school of about fifty at Penzance, Cornwall, in 1911. As a rule Pilot Whales move about in large schools composed sometimes of hundreds of individuals.

---

*This whale is not a "Royal Fish" *in Scotland*, and any carcase washed ashore *on that part of the British Islands* should not be buried at the expense of the Department of Trade.

RISSO'S DOLPHIN
Grampus griseus (Cuvier)

Length.—Up to 13 feet.

Colour.—General body colour dark grey, darkening to black on fins and tail. Lighter grey or even white on ventral surface. No well-marked boundary between darker and lighter areas. Older animals usually marked with long, narrow scars.

Form.—General body form rather robust. No distinct beak. "Forehead" bulging but less pronounced than in the Pilot Whale or False Killer. Back fin high, in mid-body length, rather acutely pointed, point backwardly directed, hinder margin concave. Flippers rather long, tapering to a point, one-sixth body length. Flukes with notch in middle of hinder edge.

Teeth.—Normally restricted to lower jaws, very occasionally one or at most two in upper jaw which otherwise toothless. Three to seven teeth on each side of lower jaw. Diameter at gum up to slightly over ½ in.

General Remarks.—Risso's Dolphin is distributed throughout the seas of the world. Since 1913 sixty-five reports have been received of British strandings. These have predominated on the south and west coasts, an indication of an Atlantic approach to British waters. Strandings on the east coast have been much fewer in number. This dolphin occurs singly or in small schools composed at most of about a dozen animals. The elongated flipper might in identification cause this species to be confused with the Pilot Whale. The general colour and more bulging "forehead" of the latter species, together with the differences in tooth arrangement make it easily distinguishable from Risso's Dolphin.

KILLER OR GRAMPUS
Orcinus orca (Linnæus)

Length.—Males up to 30 feet, females about 15 feet.

Colour.—Conspicuously black and white (sometimes yellow). Black of back distinctly defined from white of belly. Lens-shaped white patch extending backwards from just behind the eye. Ill-defined grey saddle behind back fin. Chin and throat white. Towards the tail on either side white of ventral surface extending upwards and backwards into the black of the sides. Under surface of flukes white. Flippers black on both surfaces.

Form.—General form robust. No beak from snout tip outline of head passing gradually and without break into that of the back. Back fin situated midway in body length, in females and young males moderately high, tip projecting backwards; in adult males very high (up to six feet) triangular, acutely pointed. Flippers rounded, in females and young males about one-ninth of body length, in old males about one-fifth. Tail flukes becoming greatly enlarged in old males, notch in middle of hinder edge.

Teeth.—Ten to thirteen on each side of upper and lower jaws. Diameter in adult 1 to 2 in. Flattened in front and behind so that cross-section at gum oval not circular, larger diameter across the jaw.

General Remarks.—The Killer is easily recognized by its conspicuous coloration. If, however, this should be obscured, as in a decomposing carcase, the animal can be identified by its massive teeth, only the False Killer has teeth of comparable size, but in that species (*q.v.*) the tooth root is cylindrical and the cross-section at the gum is therefore circular, not oval.

The Killer is world-wide in its distribution and has been recorded thirty-nine times on the British coasts since 1913. As its name implies it is distinguished by its great ferocity, being the only cetacean which habitually preys on other warm-blooded animals.

FALSE KILLER
Pseudorca crassidens (Owen)

Length.—Males up to 18 feet 6 in., females up to 16 feet 6 in.

Colour.—Entirely black except for white scar marks.

Form.—Head evenly rounded, without trace of beak. Back fin midway in body length, moderate size, tip pointing backwards. Flippers tapering to a point, about one-tenth body length (this distinguishing it from the Pilot Whale in which the proportion is one-fifth). Flukes with notch in middle of hinder edge.

Teeth.—Nine to eleven on each side of upper and lower jaws. Diameter at gum up to 1 in. Cross-section circular.

General Remarks.—The False Killer was originally described from a sub-fossil skeleton found in the Cambridgeshire fens. Specimens in the flesh were first recorded in this country in 1927, when a school of about 150 stranded in the Dornoch Firth, Sutherlandshire. It was subsequently reported in 1934 and 1935 when smaller numbers stranded. The species is widely distributed and numerous records exist, from various parts of the world, of the stranding of large numbers.

28

COMMON PORPOISE
Phocoena phocoena (Linnæus)

Length.—Up to 6 feet.

Colour.—Back black, belly white, sides between black of back and white of belly greyish, varying in extent. Flippers, flukes and tail stock black. Streak of black extending forwards from flippers to angle of mouth.

Form.—Snout evenly rounded, no narrow beak. Back fin about middle of back, triangular with little if any concavity of hinder margin. Flippers with rounded tip, almost oval in outline. Tail with notch in middle of posterior margin.

Teeth.—Twenty-two to twenty-seven on each side of upper and lower jaws. Diameter at gum about $\frac{1}{10}$ in.

Crowns of teeth flattened, spade-shaped, but when worn away appear like worn conical teeth of other dolphins.

General Remarks.—This is by far the commonest British species of cetacean. It is found on all parts of the coast, sometimes ascending rivers many miles from the sea. It occurs generally in the coastal waters of countries bordering the North Atlantic, in the North Sea, Baltic, White Sea and Greenland Sea. It breeds in the summer. Gestation occupies about a year and the calf when born is about half the length of the adult animal.

29

BOTTLE-NOSED DOLPHIN
Tursiops truncatus (Montagu)

Length.—Up to 12 feet.

Colour.—Back and sides from tip of snout to notch of flukes, black or dark brown. Throat and belly white, but tailwards of the vent pigmented as back. Flippers and flukes pigmented on both surfaces the pigment of flippers being continuous with that of body.

Form.—General form rather robust. Well-defined snout about 3 in. long in middle line. Dorsal fin in mid-length of body, moderately high, tip backwardly directed and rather acutely pointed, hinder edge concave. Tail stock not greatly compressed (*cf.* White sided and White-beaked Dolphins). Flukes with notch in middle of hinder edge. Flippers moderate in size, broad near the base, tapering to a rounded tip, curved lower border.

Teeth.—Twenty-two to twenty-five on each side of upper and lower jaws. Diameter at gum $\frac{3}{4}$ to $\frac{1}{2}$ in.

(NOTE.—Aged animals. which are most frequently stranded, often lack the full complement of teeth.)

General Remarks.—This species is widely distributed in the North Atlantic. In British waters, following the Common Porpoise and preceding the Common Dolphin, it is second in order of frequency of stranding, 185 having been reported since 1913; most of these were on the south and west coasts of England. It has only rarely been reported from the North Sea.

WHITE-BEAKED DOLPHIN
Lagenorhynchus albirostris Gray

Length.—9 to 10 feet.

Colour.—As indicated by common name, beak white. Back generally darkly pigmented but with longitudinal grey streaks on sides which may extend on to back behind back fin. Pigmentation of sides anterior to vent extending low down on to belly, which with lips and throat brilliantly white. Side of head behind the eye grey darkly flecked. Line of pigment joining angle of mouth and flipper insertion. Flippers black, originating within area of dark pigmentation. Tail stock and flukes dark.

Form.—General form rather robust. Beak distinct, short, about 2 in. in middle line. Dorsal fin in mid-body length, large, rounded, backwardly projecting tip, hinder margin deeply concave. Tail stock compressed so that strongly keeled above and below. Flippers broad near insertion, tapering to a rounded tip, lower margin slightly curved (*cf.* White-sided Dolphin). Flukes with notch in middle of hinder edge.

Teeth.—Twenty-two to twenty-five on each side of upper and lower jaws. Diameter about $\frac{1}{4}$ in.

General Remarks.—This is a northern species which in British waters frequents the North Sea to much greater extent than the Atlantic or English Channel coasts. It often occurs in very large schools, but as a rule only single individuals are involved in strandings. Since 1913 eighty-three of these have been recorded.

WHITE-SIDED DOLPHIN
Lagenorhynchus acutus (Gray)

Length.—9 to 10 feet.

Colour.—Darkly pigmented on back, tail and flippers. Snout dark. Dark area in region of vent. Whiteness of throat and belly extending higher up on sides than in the White-beaked Dolphin. Each flank conspicuously marked by elongated streak of lighter colour extending from below dorsal fin on to the tail stock. Flippers inserted outside pigmented region, but connected by narrow dark streak with the angle of the mouth.

Form.—General form rather robust. Beak distinct about 2 in., in middle line. Dorsal fin in mid-body length, large rounded, backwardly projecting tip, hinder margin concave. Tail stock strongly compressed so that pronounced keel above and below. Flukes with notch in middle of hinder edge. Flippers broad close to body, but tapering to a rounded tip, lower margin more curved than in White-beaked Dolphin.

Teeth.—Thirty to forty on each side of upper and lower jaws. Diameter about $\frac{3}{16}$ in.

General Remarks.—The White-sided Dolphin is common to the north of the British Isles and correlated with this most reports of its stranding have been from Orkney and Shetland. It is, however, not unknown farther south, specimens having been reported from Sligo, Yorkshire, and the Outer Hebrides. Like the White-beaked Dolphin it generally moves about in large schools. Since 1913 twenty-four strandings on the British coast have been recorded.

COMMON DOLPHIN
Delphinus delphis Linnæus

Length.—Up to 8 feet, generally about 6 feet.

Colour.—Dark colour of back not extending far down on sides. The black flippers originating from the lighter portions of sides but from their base a dark, narrowing streak extending forward to lower jaws. Eye surrounded by black circle giving off sharply defined, narrow black streak towards base of beak. Alternating streaks of dark and light pigment on sides, the uppermost dark streaks joined to the dark portion of the back below the back fin.

Form.—General form slender, graceful. Snout long, narrow and well defined from "forehead", as much as 6 in. long in middle line. Back fin in mid-body length, moderately developed, backwardly directed tip, concave hinder edge. Tail region very slender, no keels developed comparable to those of the White-sided or White-beaked Dolphins. Flukes with notch in middle of hinder edge. Flipper broad near base, tapering to rounded point, upper edge at first convex then concave, lower border curved.

Teeth.—Forty to fifty on each side of upper and lower jaws. Diameter $\frac{1}{10}$ in.

General Remarks.—Widely distributed in temperate and warm seas, the Common Dolphin, as this name implies, is one of the most abundant species in British waters; only the Common Porpoise is more often stranded. Since 1913, 135 reports have been received, mostly from the south and west coasts, less frequently from the east coast of Scotland, and very rarely from the English coast north of the Thames estuary.

N.B.—Dolphins resembling the Common Dolphin in the form of the head, but differing in colour, might occur on the British coasts. Information about these is *especially* required.

EUPHROSYNE DOLPHIN
Stenella coeruleoalba (Meyen)

Length.—Up to 7 feet.

Colour.—Darkly pigmented on back, white on belly. Narrow, dark band extending from eye along side to vent, branch given off above base of flipper, double bar of pigment from flipper insertion to eye, the lower bar not quite reaching the eye. Black pigment encircling eye. Darkly pigmented flippers inserted on the light part of body. Region of mouth pigmented.

Form.—General form slender. Very similar to, and might be mistaken for, Common Dolphin. Beak length in middle line about 5 in., sharply defined from "forehead". Back fin in mid-body length, moderately developed, rather acute and backwardly projecting tip, concave hinder edge. Flipper tapering to the tip, curved lower border, upper border at first convex, then shallowly concave. Flukes with notch in middle of hinder edge.

Teeth.—Forty-three to fifty on each side of upper and lower jaws. Diameter about $\frac{1}{8}$ in.

General Remarks. Four specimens of this dolphin have so far been recorded on the British coast, three from the south-west of England and one from north Wales. It is a typical North Atlantic species, and one about which more information is especially wanted. Its superficial similarity to the Common Dolphin makes for confusion between the two, but the difference in the pigmentation on the sides should help to distinguish them.

BRITISH MUSEUM (NATURAL HISTORY)
Other zoology publications

<table>
<thead>
<tr><th>Publication
Number</th><th>Price</th></tr>
</thead>
</table>

377. **Starfishes and their relations.** By A. M. Clark. 2nd edition. Pp. 119; 16 plates, 30 text-figures. 1968, 8vo. 75p

628. **Seals of the world.** By J. E. King. Pp. 154; 14 plates, 17 text-figures, 30 maps, frontispiece. 1964, 8vo. 75p

638. **Natural history of snakes.** By H. W. Parker. Second edition in preparation

775. **Finding and identifying mammals in Britain.** By G. B. Corbet. Pp. 56; 4 coloured plates, 74 text-figures. 1975, 8vo. ..   £1.00

761. **The cichlid fishes of Lake Victoria, East Africa:** the biology and evolution of a species flock. By P. H. Greenwood. *Bulletin of the British Museum (Natural History)* Zoology Supplement No. 6. Pp. vi+134; 1 plate, 77 text-figures. 1974, 4to.   Paperback £3.75   Boards £6.00

111. **The feeding mechanisms of a deep sea fish,** *Chauliodus sloani* **Schneider.** By V. V. Tchernavin. Pp. viii+101; 10 plates, 36 text-figures. 1953, 4to. £2.50

718. **Reports on Cetacea stranded on the British coasts,** No. 14 Cetacea stranded from 1948–1966. By F. C. Fraser. Pp. 65; 9 text-figures, 9 maps. 1974, 4to. £3.00

717. **The phyla Sipuncula and Echiura.** By A. C. Stephen and S. J. Edmonds. Pp. viii+528; 60 text-figures. 1972, 4to.   ..   £10.00

642. **A synopsis of the Siphonophora.** By A. K. Totton. Pp. viii+231; 40 plates, 156 text-figures, frontispiece. 1965, 4to.   ..   £16.50

Whales and dolphins of European seas. A 594 × 841 mm wallchart in full colour depicting all 24 species found around the British Isles.